LAB series

GEOLOGY LAB FOR KIDS

Cool Crystal Creations

EXPLORING THE WONDERS OF THE EARTH WITH SINGLE STRAND AND CRYSTAL CLUSTERS

GARRET ROMAINE

QUARRY

Brimming with creative inspiration, how-to projects, and useful information to enrich your everyday life, Quarto Knows is a favorite destination for those pursuing their interests and passions. Visit our site and dig deeper with our books into your area of interest: Quarto Creates, Quarto Cooks, Quarto Homes, Quarto Lives, Quarto Drives, Quarto Explores, Quarto Gifts, or Quarto Kids.

First Published in 2018 by Quarry Books, an imprint of The Quarto Group,
100 Cummings Center, Suite 265-D, Beverly, MA 01915, USA.
T (978) 282-9590 F (978) 283-2742 QuartoKnows.com

Quarry Books titles are also available at discount for retail, wholesale, promotional, and bulk purchase. For details, contact the Special Sales Manager by email at specialsales@quarto.com or by mail at The Quarto Group, Attn: Special Sales Manager, 401 Second Avenue North, Suite 310, Minneapolis, MN 55401, USA.

10 9 8 7 6 5 4 3 2 1

ISBN: 978-1-63159-455-7

Content for this book was originally found in *Geology Lab for Kids* by Garret Romaine (Quarry Books, 2017).

Digital edition published in 2018

Page Layout: Alex Youngblood
Photography: Patrick Smith Photography, except image by Shutterstock on cover, top right.

Printed in USA

MIX
Paper from responsible sources
FSC® C008080

CONTENTS

INTRODUCTION

Geology is the science of the Earth and learning to describe what you see so that someone else can understand. Once you get good at talking about the world around you, it's not hard to take that to the next level and figure out what happened to the Earth in the past, even if you can't see it happening today. Nobody has ever traveled to the middle of the Earth, but by making models based on places we have been, we think we know what's going on there. That's science—make a prediction, see if you can prove it, and then apply it to bigger questions.

In this book, you will learn a lot about the way things happen and why. You'll be introduced to the science behind processes you see all around you, and you'll learn to think about the Earth in new and exciting ways. Some of the most important parts of geology come down to very simple concepts—gravity, friction, heat, and water.

Geology is based on observations and predictions that are part of the scientific model. Fortunately, the Earth works in a way we can understand, so if we can make the right model, we can use what we see in that model to predict other forces. We can measure things at a small scale, and we can make models to teach others. Even simple, fun projects can show the larger world at work. The labs and projects in this book will help you understand how much fun it is to learn about the world around you.

Over the years, I have spent countless hours working with kids just like you in lectures, at demonstrations, and even as a merit badge counselor, helping them understand the world around them. Many of the labs here are time-tested, having been around for years. But some are completely new or bring a new twist to an old idea. We'll start with simple concepts and then connect the dots to bigger ideas. In that way, these labs are like building blocks: start small and keep building. At some point, you'll probably find that you are learning how more and more pieces of the puzzle fit together. That's always been the most enjoyable for me, showing others how all the different things they already know can apply. It's always a lot of fun to go to the beach and pick up a few rocks, but when you know how to identify the rocks and explain how they got there, you feel like a great detective solving a big riddle. Some of you may even go on to careers in the Earth sciences or become planetary scientists who travel to distant locales. I hope that's the case!

Let's get started. And remember: No one likes a messy lab partner!

IDENTIFYING MINERALS

Rocks and minerals are the building blocks of the Earth. Minerals have a chemical formula, with an exact number of atoms of different elements. For example, calcite is $CaCO_3$—it has one calcium atom, one carbon atom, and three oxygen atoms. Minerals can be identified with tests for streak, hardness, crystal angle, and density, which you will learn in these labs. Rocks are made up of different minerals, in lots of combinations, and they can be glued, pressed, or melted together in many ways. To identify rocks, you need to know what minerals are in them, how they are held together, and how they formed. You will also learn about the three "families" of rocks: sedimentary, igneous, and metamorphic.

Shown here are many of the most common minerals that you can find, plus a few that are rare and valuable. Most of the rocks listed here are very common. If you can learn to identify them, you can start to explain the world around you.

Minerals

Calcite

Epidote

Feldspar

Fluorite

Garnet

Gold

Gypsum

Jade

Malachite

Muscovite mica

Pyrite

Quartz

UNIT
1

SINGULAR CRYSTALS

Maybe you've heard this joke: "How do you eat an elephant?" The answer is "one bite at a time." So, how do you "build" the Earth? That's simple, too: one crystal at a time.

Crystals come in a variety of shapes that scientists call *habits*. Common crystal habits include squares, triangles, and six-sided hexagons. Usually, crystals form when liquids cool, such as when you create ice cubes. Crystals form in ways that do not allow for perfect shapes if conditions are too cold, too hot, or there isn't enough source material.

But when conditions are right, we see beautiful displays. Usually, this involves a slow, steady environment where the individual atoms have plenty of time to join and fit perfectly into what's known as the *crystal lattice*. This is the basic structure of atoms that is seen time after time. Crystals build in size when more and more atoms can find a place in the lattice to attach themselves.

In these labs, we'll create a liquid that allows the atoms plenty of time to join together. Sometimes, this involves starting with a "seed" crystal. The seed is already formed correctly and gives the atoms a chance to attach the right way. Sometimes crystals just want to form as a sheet, but we want to see the beauty of nature, so we're going to use a seed to form the crystals that we want.

LAB 1

TASTY TREATS

Build a solid sugar crystal, sometimes called rock candy.

MATERIALS

- **1 cup (236 ml) of water**
- **Pan for boiling water**
- **3+ cups (600+ g) of white sugar**
- **Metal stirring spoon**
- **3–4 drops of food coloring of any color**
- **12″ (30 cm) of rough yarn or twine**
- **Scissors**
- **6″ (15 cm) pencil**
- **½-quart (473 ml) narrow-mouth glass Mason jar**
- **Round, hard ring-shaped candy (or other clean weight)**
- **Paper towel, napkin, or washcloth**

Safety Tips

- Be cautious around the stove to avoid burns.
- Ask an adult for help boiling the water.

PROTOCOL

STEP 1: Add the water to the pan and boil the water on the stove. A microwave is not recommended.

STEP 2: Stir in the sugar slowly, adding as much as possible until it starts to build up at the bottom. Don't stop: you want your solution to be saturated.

STEP 3: Add a few drops of food coloring to make a rich color. Let cool.

STEP 4: Cut a piece of yarn or twine that is 1 inch (2.5 cm) longer than the height of your jar.

STEP 5: Tie one end of the twine or yarn around the pencil, leaving enough string to dangle the length of your jar without touching the bottom. Tie the other end around the piece of candy.

STEP 6: Moisten the string thoroughly with water, and then sprinkle lightly with sugar so that you create small "seed" crystals. Let dry for ten minutes.

STEP 7: Pour the cooled water mixture into the jar. The solution needs to be cooled so that it won't dissolve your seed crystal. Avoid pouring any of the little sugar crystals from the bottom of the pan.

STEP 8: Place the pencil across the mouth of the jar so the candy floats in the mixture.

STEP 9: Place a paper towel, napkin, or washcloth over the jar and set it aside in a corner of the kitchen. Do not disturb.

STEP 10: Check on the string after a day; it should already host small, square sugar crystals.

STEP 11: Leave the string in the solution for at least a week. You can add more solution if you want to grow bigger crystals.

Creative Enrichment

1. **What happens if you use fishing line or very smooth string?**
2. **Use a magnifying glass or hand lens to look at the hardened crystals. What shape are they? Would you call that a square or a cube?**
3. **What would happen if there were twice as much water—would the sugar ever crystallize on the string?**

THE SCIENCE BEHIND THE FUN

Growing sugar crystals is a great way to learn how saturated solutions are unstable at room temperature. The solution cannot handle any more sugar when the temperature falls, and crystals start to form. Over time, some water will evaporate, while solid sugar begins to crystallize. That's why it's important to avoid using a lid.

Sugar is a crystal with the formula $C_{12}H_{22}O_{11}$. That's twelve carbon atoms, twenty-two hydrogen atoms, and eleven oxygen atoms. They form as cubes, and their crystal "habit" is known as *cubic*. If you measure the angles with a protractor, each elbow should be 90 degrees.

If you keep adding sugar solution to the jar, you can grow enormous crystals. This is key to understanding how crystals form in the Earth. A solution that flows through cracks in the rocks will refresh the small crystals and they will keep growing. If you find small crystals in a rock, they probably didn't get a lot of time to grow. But large crystals usually tell mineralogists that growth conditions were perfect for a long time.

LAB 2

SALTY SQUARES

Grow your own perfect cube of salty perfection.

MATERIALS

- 1 cup (235 ml) of water
- 7–8 tablespoons (126–144 g) of table salt (sodium chloride, NaCl). Iodized is okay.
- Food coloring (optional)
- Piece of cardboard (optional)
- Clean, clear container
- Saucer (optional)
- 12″ (30 cm) string or fishing line (optional)
- Scissors (optional)
- Pencil or butter knife (optional)
- Paper towel or coffee filter (optional)

Safety Tips

- Don't get salt in your eyes.
- Wash hands quickly after handling salt.
- Ask an adult for help boiling the water.
- Be cautious around the cooking stove to avoid burns.

PROTOCOL

STEP 1: First make a seed crystal by pouring a small amount of saturated salt solution onto a saucer or shallow bowl. As the liquid evaporates, crystals will start to form, usually overnight. Select a single square crystal and remove it from the dish.

STEP 2: Carefully pour the saturated salt solution into a clean container (making sure no undissolved salt gets in), allow the solution to cool, and then hang the seed crystal with string in the solution from a pencil or knife placed across the top of the container. You could cover the container with a coffee filter or paper towel to keep out dust yet permit evaporation.

STEP 3: Set the container in a location where it can remain undisturbed. You are more likely to get a perfect crystal instead of a mass of crystals if you allow the crystal to grow slowly (cooler temperature, shaded location) in a place free of vibrations. It can take a week or more to get a big crystal.

Creative Enrichment

1. Experiment with different types of table salt and water. See if there is any difference in the appearance of the crystals.
2. If you are trying for the "perfect crystal" use un-iodized salt and distilled water. Impurities in either the salt or water can aid in *dislocation*, in which new crystals don't stack perfectly on top of previous crystals.
3. Make a mass of crystals by pouring the saturated salt solution into a clear container. Let it slowly evaporate. Crystals will grow on the sides of the container.

THE SCIENCE BEHIND THE FUN

The hardest part of this experiment is tying the thread around your seed crystal. But without the seed crystal, it's hard to get much more than crusty salt. The perfect seed crystal gives the extra salt in your solution perfect little places to attach to, and will keep the crystal structure growing. This is the crystal lattice we discussed earlier. Salt has a perfectly cubic crystal lattice. It measures the same distance on all sides, no matter how big or small.

Salt is pretty simple. It has one sodium atom (Na) and one chlorine atom (Cl), clustered together over and over, to form a salt molecule. Thus the formula for salt is easy: NaCl. In the crystal lattice, the atoms repeat in every direction. Where there is a Cl atom showing, an Na atom can attach, and vice versa.

Salt is mined in many ways. In some places, solar evaporation of salt water produces salt crystals. There are also underground mines in salt domes where miners scoop up salt crystals or cut slabs of hardened salt into blocks. Some specialty shops sell salt from all over the world.

LAB 3

GEMMY GOODNESS

Grow your own perfect alum crystal, ready for shaping into homemade earrings or bracelets.

MATERIALS

- $^1/_2$ cup (120 ml) of very hot water (boiling is okay but not required)
- 2 clean, 1 quart (946 ml), narrow-mouth glass Mason jars
- 2 $^1/_2$ tablespoons (45 g) of pure alum powder (potassium aluminum sulfate—you must have the right kind!)
- Metal stirring spoon
- Paper towel
- Rubber band
- 12" (30 cm) of light nylon fishing line
- Scissors
- Ruler, pencil, or single chopstick

Safety Tips

- Ask an adult for help boiling the water.
- Avoid getting the alum in your eyes. If you do, rinse them with cold water.

PROTOCOL

STEP 1: Add $^1/_2$ cup (120 ml) of hot water to a clean jar.

STEP 2: Slowly stir in the alum with the metal spoon. Add as much alum as you can until it starts to pile up on the bottom of the jar. This means your solution is saturated.

STEP 3: Cover the jar with the paper towel and use the rubber band to keep it in place. This keeps dust out of your alum solution and prevents impurities from wrecking your crystal structure.

STEP 4: Let sit overnight (sixteen hours minimum).

STEP 5: Pour the contents of the first jar into the second clean jar, leaving the residue in the first jar. Inspect this residue closely. These are small "seed" crystals that you're going to need to create a larger crystal, so make sure they are large enough to work with. If not, return the solution to the jar and wait another day.

STEP 6: Use the light nylon fishing line to tie a knot around the largest seed crystal. Do not damage the crystal. If it is too small, return to step 5 and get a larger seed crystal to work with. The more perfect your seed crystal, the better your end crystal will look.

STEP 7: Tie the other end of the line around a ruler so that you can hang the crystal completely in the alum solution. You can use a pencil or chopstick (or similar) instead. Do not let the seed crystal touch the sides of the jar or the bottom of the jar, as this will affect the crystal's shape.

STEP 8: Cover the jar again with your paper towel and rubber band. Place in a safe spot, out of the way where it can grow for many days.

STEP 9: Wait for at least a week. The longer you wait, the larger the crystal will grow. If you see small crystals starting to form on your jar, take out the crystal on the fishing line, place it back in the cleaned first jar, and pour the alum solution back in that jar as well (a fine screen might help). Don't let any of the small crystals get in, because they will compete with your big crystal for alum and it won't grow.

Creative Enrichment

1. Try using thread and growing tiny crystals all along its length.
2. Try altering the cooling rate by adding ice cubes, setting the cooling jar in a bath of ice water, or keeping the solution in a saucepan and leaving it on the stove at a very low heat.
3. You could also grow a crystal without the string, just by letting it sit in the solution.
4. Try adding some glow-in-the-dark liquid from a yellow highlighter to your solution to make a crystal that glows under UV light.

THE SCIENCE BEHIND THE FUN

Scientists call alum a hydrated potassium aluminum sulfate, with the chemical formula $KAl(SO_4)_2{*}12H_2O$. That means it has a potassium atom, K, and an aluminum atom, Al. It is a sulfate, which is sulfur and oxygen, and it is hydrated, meaning it has water molecules, in this case, twelve.

Alum was used by the ancients to purify water, because it attaches to silt and solids, which either float or sink. Today, it is used to stop bleeding, in deodorants, and for pickling. It is known as *Fitkari* in India and *tawas* in parts of Asia.

Alum can grow into large isometric crystals that resemble two pyramids stacked at the base. As long as fresh solution continues to flow into an area where crystals have started, crystals can grow. It is a simple crystal to grow at room temperature, and its faces can make attractive, inexpensive jewelry.

UNIT 2

CRYSTAL CLUSTERS

Having one crystal is great, but that's not usually how the Earth works, and having a lot of them together is even more fun. Crystal clusters are a lot easier to enjoy, because you won't need a magnifying glass to see them, like you would with some individual crystals.

In nature, crystals usually form together because there is more than enough material. Crystals generally start as a liquid, and then cool down slowly enough to form proper "faces" on their crystal structure. Sometimes we get the right conditions to create veins, which can occasionally host rich zones of gold, silver, or other metal ores. In other conditions, these veins form small pockets of gems such as rubies, emeralds, and sapphires. A term you should know is *vug*—a pocket or gap in a vein where bigger crystals can form. Many of the most valuable gems grow in vugs, where conditions are often perfect to slowly form larger, better crystals.

LAB 4

CRUSTY CRYSTALS

Create your own crystals around whatever structure you think up.

MATERIALS

- Pipe cleaners
- 1-quart (946 ml) wide-mouth glass Mason jar
- 12″ (30 cm) string or fishing line
- Scissors
- Ruler, pencil, or single chopstick
- 1 quart (946 ml) of water
- Borax, sugar, or salt
- Long wooden spoon for stirring
- Blue (or another color) food coloring

Safety Tips

- Wash your hands after working with Borax.
- Ask an adult for help boiling the water.
- Be cautious around the stove to avoid burns.

PROTOCOL

STEP 1: Using pipe cleaners, create a framework of any shape—snowflake, square, pyramid, circle, etc.

STEP 2: Make sure that the shape can easily fit through the mouth of the wide-mouthed jar without having to squeeze through. If it can't, trim the sides down.

STEP 3: Cut a 6" (15 cm) length of string and attach it to one side of your pipe cleaner shape. Tie the other end of the string to a ruler, pencil, or chopstick. Make sure your framework hangs into the jar but doesn't come close to touching the bottom (leave about an inch [2.5 cm] of room). Once your length is set, tie the knots and remove the shape from the jar.

STEP 4: Bring a pot with about a quart (946 ml) of water to a boil and pour about 3 cups (709 ml) of the hot liquid into the jar. Add 3 tablespoons (54 g) of Borax, sugar, or salt per each cup (235 ml) of water, so about 9 tablespoons (162 g). Stir it up, but don't worry if some Borax, sugar, or salt settles to the bottom of the jar.

STEP 5: If you want a colored crystal cluster, stir in some food coloring. You will have a little trouble seeing your shape as the crystals grow on it if you use a lot of food coloring. Now pour the mixture into the jar.

STEP 6: Use the string to hang the pipe cleaner framework in the jar, with the stick resting on top of the jar. Make sure that you've added enough solution to completely submerge the pipe cleaner.

STEP 7: Put the jar somewhere where it is safe from being disturbed. Leave it alone and let the science work without bumping it.

STEP 8: If you used Borax, you should have a nice cluster of crystals everywhere on the framework, and even on the string, by the next day. Sugar will take a little longer, and salt is the slowest (it could take two or three days).

Creative Enrichment

1. **Try twisting your pipe cleaners into flowers, snowflakes, or other forms.**

THE SCIENCE BEHIND THE FUN

Mixing the dry chemical with the water created a super-saturated suspension. A *suspension* is a mixture that contains solid particles large enough to settle out. By mixing the chemical into hot water, it stays suspended longer. If you used colder water, you would not be able to add as much dry chemical before it began to settle.

As the liquid begins to cool, it starts to crystallize. You'll see this crystallization on both the bottom of the jar and on your pipe cleaner. The solution continues to make a crust on top of your framework and on top of other crystals until you pull it out of the water.

Borax, also known as sodium tetraborate, is a term for a common salt with the formula $Na_2B_4O_7 \cdot 10H_2O$. The *B* is for *boron*. Borax forms from evaporation of boron-rich waters, especially seasonal lakes, such as in Southern California and Nevada deserts.

LAB 5

CRYSTAL GARDEN

The charcoal crystal garden is a classic crystal-growing project, because it's fun to watch grow. You can experiment with colors, too.

MATERIALS

- **Charcoal briquettes, cardboard, or pieces of sponge or porous rock**
- **Glass dish or shallow bowl (non-metal)**
- **Hammer (optional)**
- **Water, preferably distilled**
- **1-quart (946 ml) wide-mouth glass Mason jar**
- **Table salt (sodium chloride)**
- **Ammonia**
- **Laundry bluing agent**
- **Food coloring**

Safety Tips

- Always wash your hands after using the chemicals.
- Get an adult to help you with the chemicals.
- The components of the garden are not edible, so adult supervision is recommended.

PROTOCOL

STEP 1: Gather your materials.

STEP 2: Place chunks of your *substrate* (i.e., cardboard, charcoal briquette, sponge, cork, brick, porous rock) in an even layer in the non-metal dish or bowl. You want small pieces, so you may need to (carefully) use a hammer to break the material up.

STEP 3: Sprinkle water, preferably distilled, onto the substrate until it has been thoroughly dampened. Pour off and discard any excess water.

STEP 4: In an empty jar, mix 3 tablespoons (54 g) un-iodized salt, 3 tablespoons (45 ml) ammonia, and 6 tablespoons (90 ml) bluing agent. Stir the mixture until the salt is dissolved.

STEP 5: Pour the mixture over the substrate layer (over the cardboard, brick, sponge, etc.).

STEP 6: Add and swirl a bit of water around in the empty jar to pick up the remaining chemicals and pour this liquid onto the substrate, too.

STEP 7: Dot drops of food coloring here and there across the surface of the garden. Areas with no food coloring will be white.

STEP 8: Sprinkle more salt (about 2 tablespoons [28 g]) across the surface of the garden.

STEP 9: Allow your garden to grow in an area where it will not be disturbed.

STEP 10: On days 2 and 3, pour a mixture of ammonia, water, and bluing agent (2 tablespoons [30 ml] each) in the bottom of the pan. Avoid pouring liquid on the delicate growing crystals.

STEP 11: Keep the pan in an undisturbed place, but check on it periodically. Let it grow until you are pleased with its appearance. Enjoy!

Creative Enrichment

1. Bluing agent is found in the laundry aisles of some grocery stores. If you can't find bluing agent at a store near you, it is available online.

2. The crystals grow quickly for this project because the substrate (charcoal or whatever you chose) has a large surface area. Crystals start to form on the porous materials and then grow as capillary action draws more fluid up from the dish. Water evaporates on the surface, depositing solids/forming crystals, and pulling more solution up from the base of the dish.

THE SCIENCE BEHIND THE FUN

This experiment combines the crystal growing methods we've been performing with a property of charcoal. Because charcoal is porous, it sucks up the water at just the right rate for the crystals to grow. The crystals are very delicate, almost dust. Use a magnifying glass or a hand lens to look closely at them.

LAB 6

NEST OF NEEDLES

Build your own spiky crystals, atom by atom, so you can learn crystal structure.

MATERIALS

- **Small bowl, mug, or disposable plastic container**
- **Hot water**
- **Metal stirring spoon**
- **Epsom salt**
- **Food coloring**

Safety Tips

- Wash your hands carefully after working with the Epsom salt and avoid getting it in your eyes. Epsom salt is used for medicinal baths, so it isn't bad for your skin, but it can irritate your eyes.
- Use warm, but not scalding, water.

PROTOCOL

STEP 1: Add ½ cup (120 ml) of hot tap water to a bowl, mug, or disposable plastic container.

STEP 2: Add a drop or two of food coloring.

STEP 3: Begin stirring in ½ cup (115 g) of Epsom salt with a metal spoon. (A wooden spoon will soak up the chemical, so don't use one. Plastic may stain, so avoid those, too.) Add the salt slowly. Toward the end, you may see salt going to the bottom of the container. This means the solution is saturated—the water cannot hold any more salt.

STEP 4: Put the container in the refrigerator for at least four hours.

STEP 5: Remove the container and pour off any extra liquid. The longer you leave the container to crystallize, the longer the crystals will grow.

Creative Enrichment

1. What happens when you grow the crystals in warm air instead of in the refrigerator? Does the experiment take more time or less time?
2. What happens when you add more solution? Do you get more crystals, or do you produce a mass?
3. What happens when you add more solution but use a different color? Do you get a mix of colors?

THE SCIENCE BEHIND THE FUN

Epsom salt has a chemical formula of $MgSO_4$—one magnesium atom, one sulfur atom, and four oxygen atoms. It gets its name from a spring in England, where people soaked in it to relieve aching muscles and joints. Today it is still used as a bath salt and in farming.

These salts attract water to the point that it can be difficult to get an accurate measurement by weight, as the crystals constantly pull moisture from the air. This experiment uses rapid evaporation. Because you used hot water to hold your liquid solution of salt, you could saturate the liquid to the point where no more salt would dissolve. Once the temperature began to drop, the solution began to freeze. But instead of freezing like water, the solution crystallized more dramatically, sending spikes in every direction.

Since there are so many small, dissolved crystals in your solution, you don't need a seed crystal for the process to begin. Once water starts to evaporate, the salt crystals start growing. They build themselves from the bottom, so it's common to end up with a real nest of needles.

Unfortunately, these crystals aren't to be used in jewelry because they break easily. They don't taste good, either. But this experiment gives fast results, so it's a great way to start learning about crystals.

Disposal of the crystals is easy: just rinse out the bowl. Food coloring could stain a plastic container, so it might be easier to rinse it and recycle it.

LAB 7

GEODES OF FUN

Make a cluster of geodes from common kitchen chemicals. This experiment calls for alum, but you can use Borax in the same proportions as the Crusty Crystals lab on page 15, or use salt in the same proportion as in the Salty Squares lab on page 10.

MATERIALS

- **Plastic eggs or small plastic bowls**
- **1-quart (1 L) of boiling water**
- **Mixing bowl or 1-quart (946 ml) wide-mouth glass Mason jar**
- **2½ tablespoons (45 g) of pure alum powder (potassium aluminum sulfate—you must have the right kind!)**
- **Long wooden spoon for stirring**
- **Set of food coloring**
- **Superglue—don't use water-soluble glues**

Safety Tips

- Avoid getting solutions in your eyes.
- Wash hands after using the chemicals.
- Ask an adult for help boiling the water.
- Be cautious around the cooking stove to avoid burns.

PROTOCOL

STEP 1: Make sure your plastic bowls or plastic eggs are clean. Note that you can also use actual eggshells if they are large enough, and *very* clean. Then you can break them away when you're done if your crystals are thick enough.

STEP 2: Bring a quart (1 L) of water to a boil and pour about 3 cups (709 ml) of the hot liquid into a mixing bowl or Mason jar. Add 2½ tablespoons (45 g) of alum per each cup of water, so if you want to make a lot of geodes, keep that ratio. Stir it up, but don't worry if some alum settles to the bottom of the jar.

STEP 3: If you want a colored crystal cluster, stir in plenty of food coloring.

STEP 4: Put a few drops of glue in the bowl or egg, coating the inside edge. Before it dries, sprinkle in some alum, Borax, or salt crystals. These are the seed crystals that will help the geode grow faster.

STEP 5: Pour the mix into the plastic bowls or eggs. If you're using eggs, use a towel, a muffin tin, or empty egg container to hold the eggs upright.

STEP 6: Put the cooling forms somewhere where they are safe from spills.

STEP 7: After twenty-four hours, you should see a crust forming. It will take some time for all the water to evaporate, but if you don't want to wait that long, you can pour the remaining liquid into a jar and reuse it for more fun later.

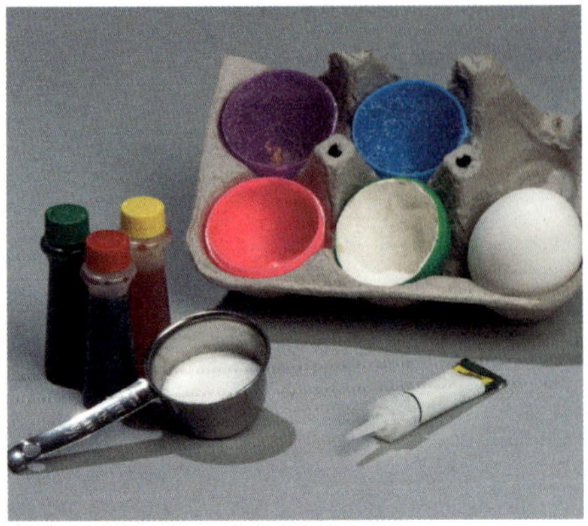

Creative Enrichment

1. Add fluorescent, glowing paint to your mix if you want to create a "space rock" effect.

THE SCIENCE BEHIND THE FUN

Geodes form in igneous and sedimentary rocks as hollow, round structures. They may begin as large bubbles or holes in the rock. Hot, quartz-rich fluids in the rocks can then reach the bubbles and start filling them in. Sometimes the hot fluids pick up colors from the rocks around them and leave colored agate bands inside the geodes.

Geodes often look like ordinary rocks on the outside. Because they cool slowly and evenly, crystals can form into fantastic shapes on the inside. The geodes also get refreshed with new surges of hot liquid, usually quartz, but other minerals, such as calcite, may come in. Sometimes the new material comes into the geode as a gas, so each crystal clinging to the inside of the geode can grow a little. Other times, the material comes in as a liquid, and the geode fills up with bands, from the bottom up.

Geodes and "thundereggs" are common in many parts of the U.S. where there is lots of lava, such as at Oregon's famed Richardson's Ranch or Keokuk, Iowa. Cracking open a geode is a lot of fun, because you never know what's inside. There are many different websites where you can order your own geodes to break apart.

UNIT 3

SPECIMEN SLEUTH

Now that we've built our own individual crystals and watched them grow in groups, it's time to study them. There are several tests that help set minerals apart, such as hardness, color, crystal angles, and density. By learning how to use these simple tests, we can narrow down the list of likely suspects when trying to identify something we don't know.

Using a system is important, because scientists have identified more than 10,000 minerals on Earth. Most are very rare, and some only occur under special conditions. More are discovered all the time, and it's still possible that you could discover a rare, unknown mineral and put your name on it. Try adding "-ite" at the end of your last name; if it sounds good, you can do an Internetsearch and see if it already exists!

The most common minerals that make up the Earth's crust have been known for a long time. If you can learn the basics about how to become a crystal detective, you can identify and investigate clues about the world around you.

LAB 8

SCRATCH THE SURFACE

Find as many items as you can and build a list of materials that can or can't scratch each other.

MATERIALS

- Penny
- Pottery
- Porcelain tile
- Glass
- Nail
- Your fingernail
- A knife
- Crystals—pyrite, calcite, gypsum, quartz, etc.
- Lab notebook and pen or pencil

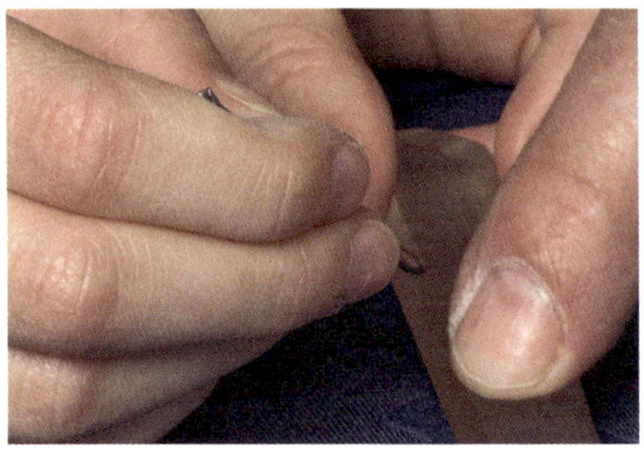

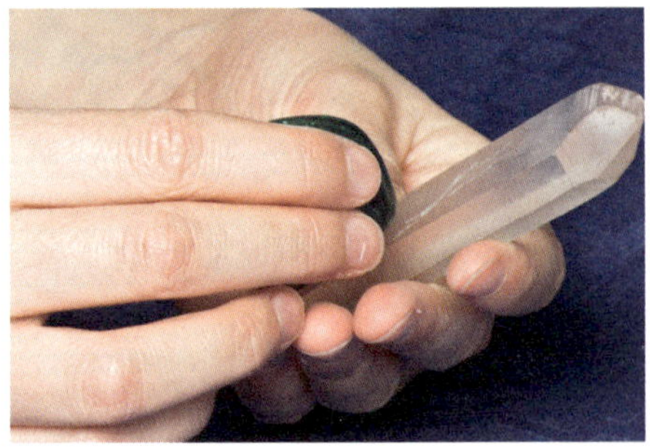

Safety Tips

- Sharp edges—don't cut yourself!

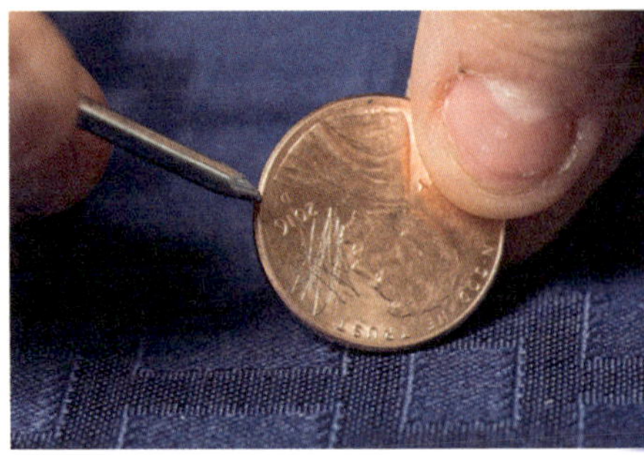

PROTOCOL

The idea here is to gather materials and try to scratch them. If you don't have any minerals, you can use things from around the house. Make a list and see if you can rank the materials by what they can and can't scratch.

Creative Enrichment

1. Try using a steel nail to scratch several different pennies—they are all a little different, but in general, older pennies are harder. Try other coins as well.
2. See if you can scratch a penny with a piece of glass or a different type of metal, such as a brass nail or screw.
3. Use a quartz crystal to try to scratch glass, coins, or steel.
4. Try other materials around the house, such as pottery, metal rulers, or older cookware.
5. Try scratching chalk, a penny, or piece of pottery with your fingernail.

THE SCIENCE BEHIND THE FUN

In 1812, the *Mohs' scale of mineral hardness* was devised by the German mineralogist Friedrich Mohs (1773–1839), who selected the ten minerals because they were common or readily available. The scale is not linear, but it makes it easy to understand which materials are harder and softer. It runs from one through ten, with talc at one as the softest and diamonds standing alone at number 10—nothing can scratch a diamond.

Hardness is a function of a material's crystal lattice. Every collector needs to know the Mohs' scale, because it is an important field test. You can carry around a few common items and quickly zero in on a mineral's identification this way.

Notice how the fingernail is useful for comparison. Here's the list you should come up with from the lab:

YOUR LIST	
Mohs' Scale	**Material Comparison**
1	Talc
2	Calcite
2.5	Fingernail
3	Gypsum
2.5–3	Gold, Silver
3–3.5	Common pottery
3	Copper penny
4–5	Iron
5.5	Knife blade
6–7	Fine pottery
6–7	Glass
6.5	Pyrite crystal
6.5–7	Porcelain
7	Quartz crystal
7+	Hardened steel file

LAB 9

STREAKS OF MYSTERY

Learn how to use common porcelain tile to find the distinctive color of powdered minerals.

MATERIALS

- **Porcelain tile—a broken piece of white tile is perfect**
- **Various coins and/or metals**
- **Hematite (optional)**
- **Malachite (optional)**
- **Azurite (optional)**

Safety Tips

- Avoid scratching yourself with sharp porcelain edges.
- Avoid breathing in the powder you create on your streak plate.

PROTOCOL

STEP 1: Locate a clean edge on your piece of porcelain.

STEP 2: Drag the material you want to test across the porcelain and note the color of the powdered streak you leave behind. You may have to push down hard.

STEP 3: Test different materials, such as nails, coat hangers, and copper wire.

Creative Enrichment

1. What happens when you try to get a streak from an agate or petrified wood?
2. Is it possible to get a streak from a diamond?
3. What can you say is the science behind using a pencil on paper?

THE SCIENCE BEHIND THE FUN

Porcelain is actually quite hard—about seven on the Mohs' scale. Thus, it is harder than most materials you want to test, and it will grind the material into a powder. Powdered material is "fresh," meaning it hasn't yet oxidized or weathered due to moisture, sunlight, or chemical reaction to water.

If you don't have the minerals listed, you can still experiment with streaks using what you have around the house. Most metals are softer than porcelain, and produce a good streak. When you find a metal that is harder than porcelain, you create a porcelain powder!

Most metallic objects like coins are a combination of different metals. Pure copper is too soft to make a good coin, so the mint adds strengthening metals to get coins that will stand up during circulation. Even gold leaves a streak. Good jewelers can usually tell how much silver is present in a gold sample just from the color, which will be less of a golden hue and more gray or silvery depending on how much silver is present. But don't wreck good jewelry just for the sake of science!

LAB 10

CRYSTAL GEOMETRY

Learn how to determine a crystal's angle. You can even use the crystals that you made in Unit 1.

MATERIALS

- **Ruler**
- **Protractor**
- **Crystal samples, such as quartz, pyrite, calcite, feldspar, mica, or the alum and other crystals you made in Unit 1**
- **Lab notebook and pen or pencil**
- **Hand lens (optional)**

Safety Tips

- Avoid sharp edges on crystal faces.

PROTOCOL

STEP 1: Build a *goniometer* by placing the ruler at the center of the protractor, with 2 inches (5 cm) of the ruler extending below the protractor.

STEP 2: Place your crystal sample with one face along the bottom of the protractor, and one face along the ruler, so that you can measure one of the angles.

STEP 3: Record the various angles until you have a full set of measurements.

STEP 4: Repeat for different crystals, until you have built a full table.

Creative Enrichment

1. What other minerals around the house can you measure?
2. How can you measure pictures of crystals you find online?
3. A material such as obsidian has no crystal structure. Do you know why?

THE SCIENCE BEHIND THE FUN

The goniometer dates back to 1538, when it was described by Dutch mathematician Gemma Frisius, who was studying navigation and surveying. One of his students, Gerardus Mercator, made a famous early map of the Earth called the Mercator Projection. Nobel prize-winning German physicist Max von Laue used a goniometer in 1912 to explore the atomic structure of crystals. Crystals have a distinctive, measureable angle to their appearance. No matter the size of the specimen, if you can measure its angles, those numbers should be the same.

Once you practice how to measure crystal angles, you can start to identify them by eye, without using a tool. For example, pure calcite crystals form a slightly tilted cube called a rhombohedron, with four angles on each two-dimensional face: 74 degrees, 106 degrees, 74 degrees, and 106 degrees, which add up to 360 degrees. Salt forms a perfect cube, with four angles of 90 degrees.

The next step is to learn to identify crystal habits—the common form a mineral adopts. There are seven common crystal habits: cubic, tetragonal, hexagonal, trigonal, orthorhombic, monoclinic, triclinic, and amorphous (no crystal structure, like glass). Once you start making a list of all the angles that you learn, you'll start to memorize them and then recognize them when you see them in the field. Geologists and mineralogists learn the angles and spot them even under a hand lens.

LAB 11

DIVINING DENSITY

Learn how to determine a mineral's density, sometimes called *specific gravity*, by measuring how heavy it is in relation to how much space it takes up. You can use your measurement as another way to identify a mineral, because almost every mineral has a slightly different density.

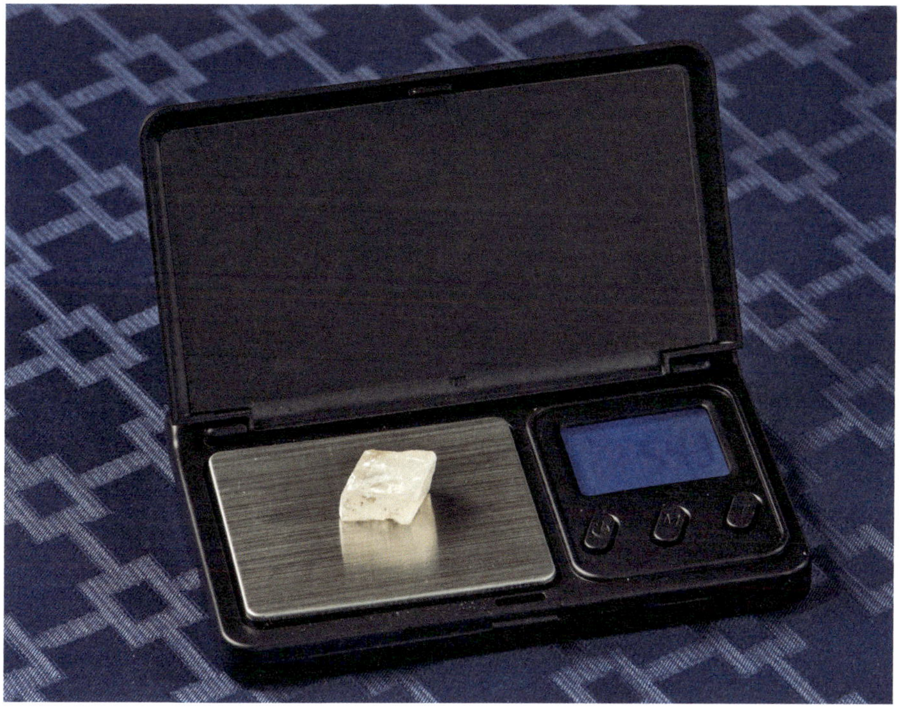

MATERIALS

- **Small digital scale, up to 10.5 oz (300 g)**
- **Small mineral specimen, such as calcite or quartz**
- **Lab notebook and pen or pencil**
- **Small plastic container, such as a margarine tub**
- **Water**
- **Paper clip or piece of wire**

Safety Tips

- **Don't cut yourself straightening or bending the paper clip.**

PROTOCOL

STEP 1: Zero out your digital scale.

STEP 2: Weigh your specimen dry and record the weight in your laboratory notebook.

STEP 3: Fill your plastic tub about three-quarters full with water.

STEP 4: Place the tub and water on your scale and suspend the paper clip in it, then zero the scale.

STEP 5: Wrap the paper clip around your specimen.

STEP 6: Suspend your mineral in the water. Do not allow the specimen to touch the sides of the tub or the bottom of the tub. Record the new weight.

STEP 7: Divide the larger number by the smaller number. Compare your specific gravity measurement against a reference such as the minerals database at www.mindat.org for your mineral and see how close you got.

Creative Enrichment

1. **How can you measure larger objects?**

THE SCIENCE BEHIND THE FUN

Mineralogists use a "key" to identify minerals, sorting samples by color, luster, streak, hardness, and density, among other characteristics. Field geologists use the term *heft* to guess density. If you pick up a rock in your hand and drop your hand a little, then raise it back up, you can feel how heavy it is naturally. But in the lab, you can get an exact reading that will let you compare against other rocks and minerals that aren't the same size. A pure sample should have a characteristic density.

Density is mass divided by volume. The key to understanding density is that you are measuring weight for a standard volume: 1 cubic centimeter. Unless you are working with a cube or a rectangle, it's hard to use math to learn the volume.

Another way to measure volume is to put the sample in a measuring glass and see how much higher the water level moves. This is called *displacement* and it takes a lot of practice to do it right. When you are using very small rocks, the difference in the water level is hard to see. This lab makes it easy to measure density, even for small specimens—but you can't measure a mineral that will dissolve.

According to legend, the Greek scholar Archimedes discovered the concept of displacement when he got into a full bathtub and watched the water overflow. He used that knowledge to determine density.

RESOURCES

Earth Science Week classroom activities

www.earthsciweek.org/classroom-activities

Check here for many more Earth science labs you can do at home.

Kids.gov

kids.usa.gov/teens/science/geology/index.shtml

You'll find many more labs that explain geology and Earth science.

The National Crystal Growing Competition

http://www.cheminst.ca/outreach/crystal-growing-competition

Canadian high school students can grow their own crystals and compete for cash prizes.

ABOUT THE AUTHOR

Garret Romaine has been an avid rock hound, fossil hunter, and gold prospector for 35 years. He is a long-time journalist, columnist, and technical writer who teaches technical writing at Portland State University. He is a Fellow in the Society for Technical Communication, an organization dedicated to explaining complex technology and science. He holds a degree in geology from the University of Oregon and a degree in geography from the University of Washington. He is the author of many books on geology and the outdoors, including *The Modern Rockhounding and Prospecting Handbook, Rockhounding Idaho, Gem Trails of Oregon, Gem Trails of Washington,* and *Gold Panning the Pacific Northwest*. He is a member of the Board of Directors for the Rice Northwest Museum of Rocks and Minerals and also serves on the board of the North American Research Group, devoted to amateur paleontologists.

ACKNOWLEDGMENTS

I'd like to thank photographer Patrick F. Smith for his patience in turning his photography studio into a science laboratory for two months, while we fine-tuned the labs and brought them to life.